D1799735

Influencing Tools for Leadership Impact essentials

By Jim Peal, PhD

Published by
Leadership Development Group
Oakland CA
Tel. (01) 805-966-3323

Copyright 2017 by Jim Peal, Ph.D.

ISBN 978-1976429156

Notes

What creates impact?

Our Focus
What & How

4

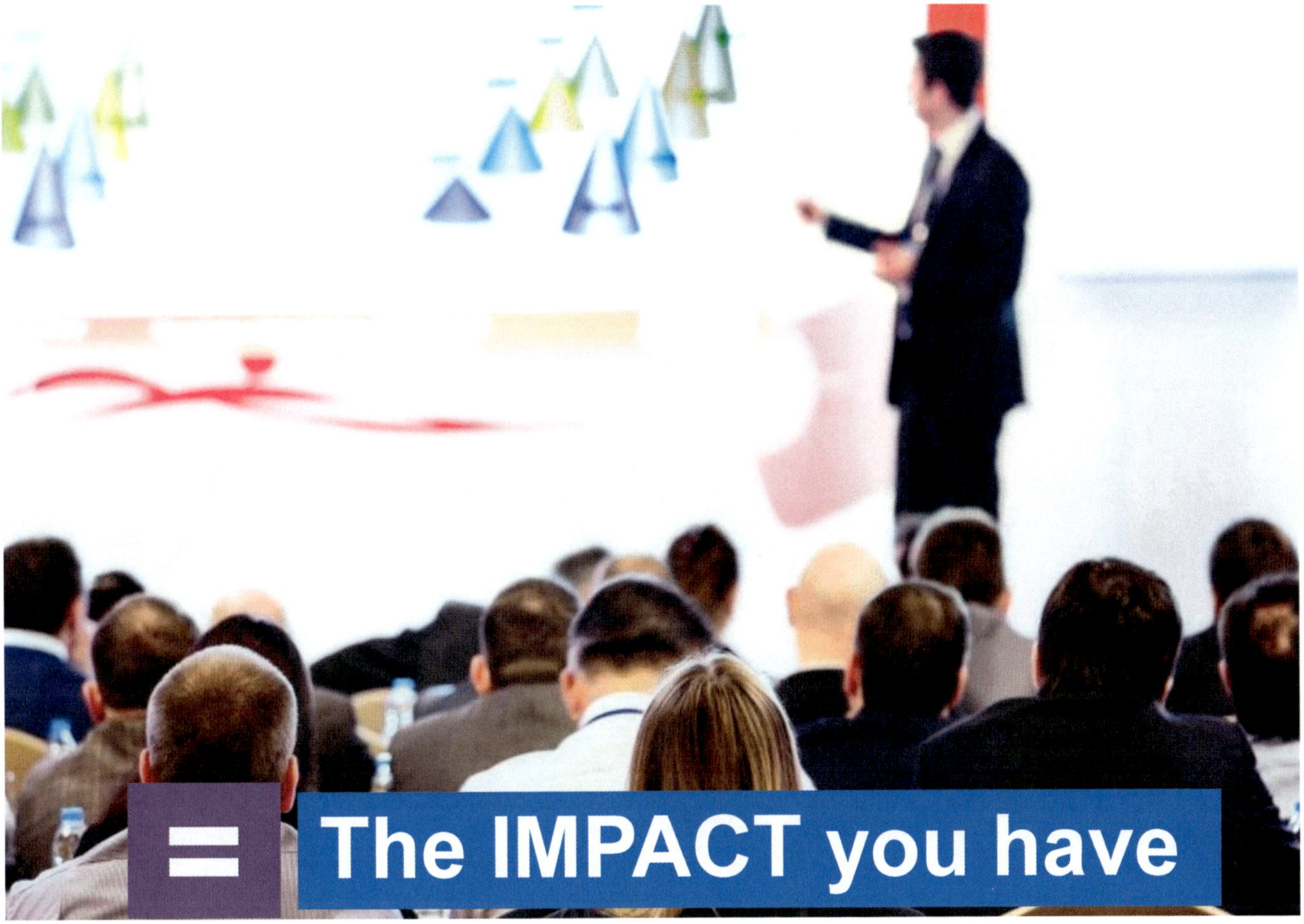

1 **Be Prepared**
Know your outcomes, material, & your audience

2 **Be Present**
Connect with your audience pay attention, respond & stay flexible

3 **Be Engaged**
Bring in your full energy, animate your topic, take them on a journey

6

Maximize Your Investment!

- Participate **100%** full out
- Support each other
- Be willing to make mistakes
- Be open to discovery
- Have fun
- Confidentiality

Outcomes

Regarding Presentations:

1. What do you do well?
2. What can you be better at?
3. What would you like to learn? Skills to master?
4. What are the take-aways you want to have?
5. How do you want to develop professionally?

1. I am relatively good at delivering technical presentations (lecturing)

2. I could be better at convincing people regarding a concept during a presentation.

3. · Do gestures better.
   · Be able to tell who is not with me/does not get me
   · How to fix bullet point ii.

5. I do not know yet: Start with technical and see if I want to stay.

Reaching Mastery

1. **Unconscious Incompetence**

   You don't know what you don't know how to do

2. **Conscious Incompetence**

   You know that you don't know how to do it

3. **Conscious Competence**

   You can do it, You have to think about what you are doing

4. **Unconscious Competence**

   You can do it without having to think about it

10

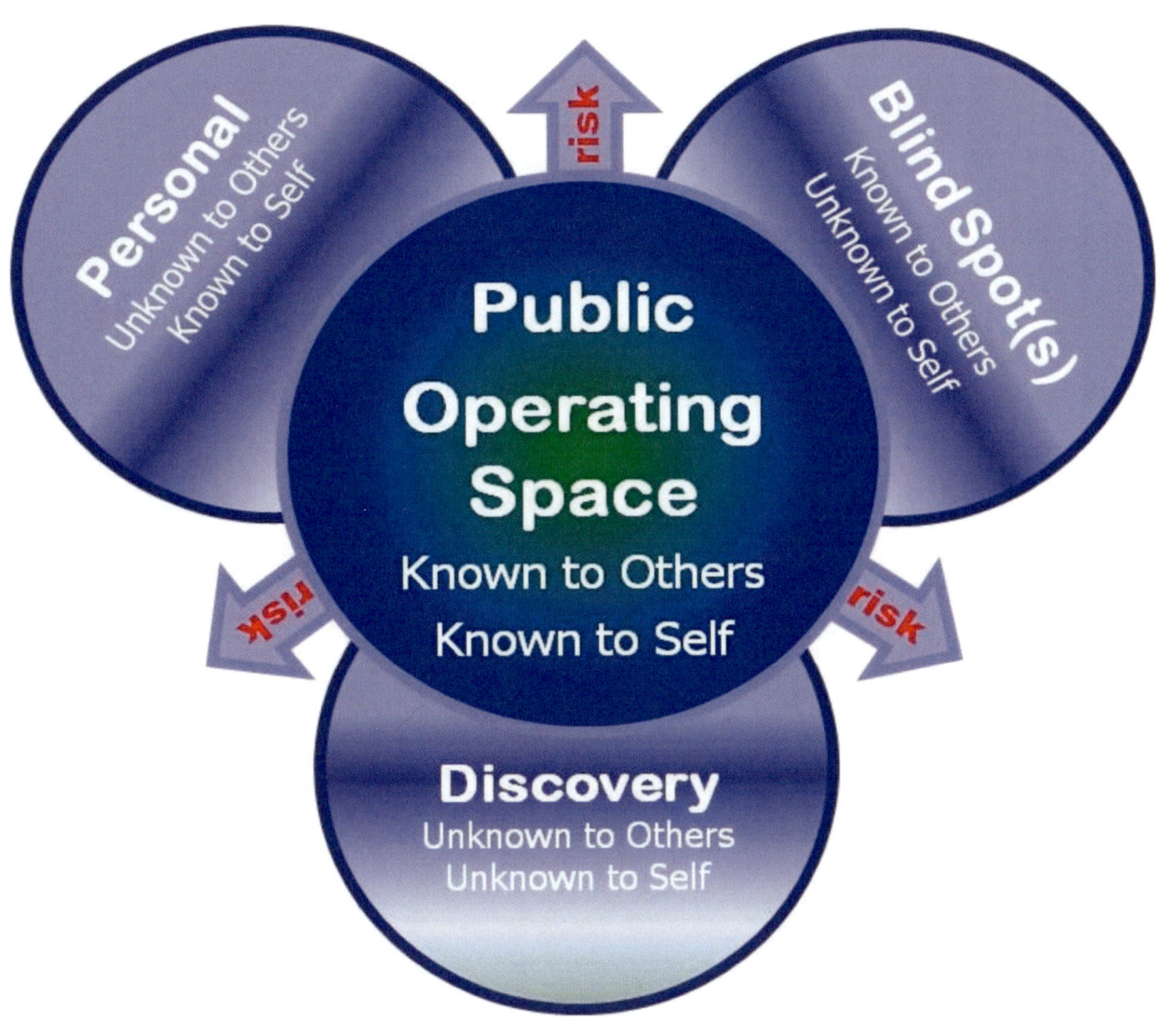

How do you like to **Receive**?
Corrective Feedback

12

Plain
Give me a hug, tell me what I did wrong, give me another hug

Open Face

What you thought I was trying to accomplish, what I did, the impact. Give me suggestions

Club
Just the meat. Be direct

Feedback Menu

Submarine
Let's sit down for a couple of hours and work out all the details

Finger

Small digestible pieces

Reinforce
positives

What you liked, What was effective, Avoid saying **"but"**

Give behavioral
suggestions

Show them with your example

14

Express passion for
Your work

- Tune into your self
- Let your natural passion and expression come through
- Energize your audience

Presence & Authenticity

Everybody is a

genius

But if you judge a fish by its
ability to climb a tree

It will live its whole life
believing that it is stupid

Albert Einstein

16

Presentation

Share:

- Your top 3 values

- What those words mean to you specifically

- Your process to come up with your top 3

- How/when each value came to be a value for you

- How do your values connect with and get expressed in the work that you do?

Your top 3 Values

Step 1. In the context of your **life** (not just work):
Circle the <u>ten</u> values that are the most important to you as guides for how to behave, or as components of a valued way of **life**. <u>Add</u> your own words to this list if you like.
Step 2. You only get five. Select the top five. Select the top four, three, two, one. Notice your process of how you went from 10 to 1.
Step 3. Look at the top three

Challenging Problems 2. Inclusion / Friendship 3. Honesty / Trust / Integrity)

What do they mean to you, exactly?
What people and or life events lead to forming your values? Think of life experiences/stories about you when you were growing up that illustrates how you formed your top 3 values.
Step 4. How do your values get expressed in your work? When you are at home? How you communicate? Deal with conflict? When you are under pressure?

I. At work : 1. ; 2; 3.
II. At home : 1; 3
III. Communicate
IV. Conflict : 1; 2
V. Under pressure : 1

Achievement	Financial gain	Physical challenge
Accountability/Responsibility	Freedom	Pleasure
Acknowledgement	✗ Friendships	Power and Authority
Advancement	Fun	Privacy
Adventure	Growth	Public service
Affection (caring)	Health	Purity
Appreciation	Helping others	Quality of what I take part in
Arts	✽ Honesty	Quality relationships
✽ Challenging problems	Humor	Respect
Change and Variety	Improvement	Religion
Choice	✽ Inclusion	Reputation
Close relationships	Independence	Results
Communication	Influencing others	Security
Community	Inner harmony	Self-Respect
Competition	Integrity	Serenity
Conformity	Intellectual status	Service
Control	Involvement	Sophistication
Cooperation	Job tranquility	Spiritual Focus
Country	Knowledge	Stability
Creativity	Leadership	Status
Decisiveness	Leisure	Supervising others
Democracy	Learning	✽ Teaching
Ecological awareness	Location	Thinking
Economic security	Love	Time freedom
Effectiveness	Loyalty	Transformation
Efficiency	Magic	Tranquility
Ethical practice	Meaningful work	Truth
Excellence	Merit	✽ Trust
Excitement	Money	Urgency
Expertise	Nature	Wealth
Faith	Being around people who are	Winning
Fame	open and honest	Wisdom
Family	Order	Work under pressure
Fast living	Patience	Work with others
Fast-paced work	Personal development	Working alone

PowerPoint
Presentation Principles

Your slides are not your **Presentation...** YOU ARE!

One picture is worth a
thousand words
Use pictures

Remember
PowerPoint
is not **Word**

Don't explain every

little thing

Make them ask

questions

Presentation Structure

Presentation Criteria

The What

- Organization of material
- Logic
- Command of material
- Framework
- Opening – high impact
- Frame
- WIIFM – *what is in for me*
- 3 Key points
- Call to action

The How

- Confidence
- Presence
- Congruency
- Animation
- Rapport
- Responsive to audience
- Posture
- Gestures
- Vocalics – clarity, projection, dynamic range
- Sensory language
- Use of stage - position
- Humor

= OVERALL

Maximize your
Impact

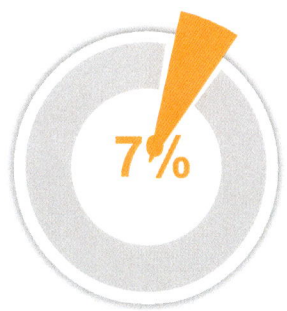 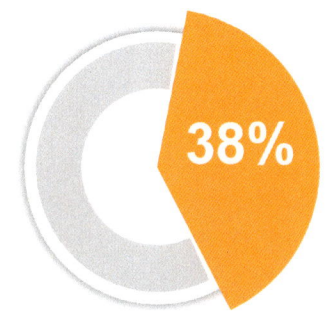 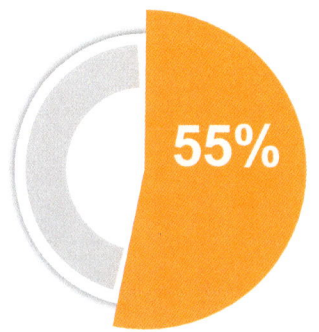

| **Digital**- Words | **Analog**- How words are spoken | **Analog**- Body language |

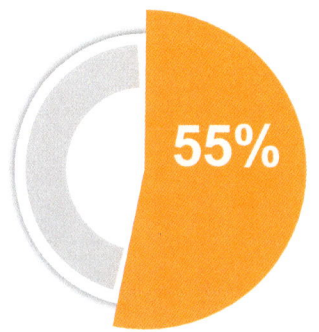

Vocalics

Your voice is one of the key carriers of your message. You can engage or turn off your audience with your voice.

- Create a resonance and dynamic range in your voice
  - Location
  - Breathing
- Use inflection intentionally
  - Command – down
  - Question – up
- Use sensory words to lead
- Use pauses for impact
- Synchronize with gestures

- Use triangles and squares
  - Feet in a V
  - Shoulders & head square
  - Back upright
  - Knees flexible
- Lean IN
  - You are looking at them vs. them looking at you
- Look people straight in the eyes 90% of the time.
- Talk to one person at a time.

31

- Brings your presentation to life
- Anchors your audience in what is important/not important
- Create a memorable association
- Make your gestures:
  - Intentional
  - Distinct and unique
- Don't:
  - Let your gestures run out of gas
  - Fidgit
  - Stick your hands in your pockets (unless that is a gesture)

Position

Your stage is 3 dimensional

- Mark key points by stepping forward
- Step back for questions – up inflection
- Mark past, present, future
    - Their future is to your left
- Move closer to understand & connect - subjective
- Step back to get the meta-view – objective
- Utilize Proxemics
    - 0 – 18" Intimate
    - 18" – 4' Personal
    - 4' – 12' Social
    - 12' - 25' Public

Organizing your
Material

Begin with the end in mind

1. Who is in your audience?

2. Where are they coming from?

3. What do you want your audience to think, feel and/or do as a results of engaging them?

4. What experience do you want to create for them?

5. What is the journey you intend to take them on?

Make Your Meeting$ Count

- Decision Making
- Project Kick-off
- Progress Updates
- Briefing & Debriefing
- Announcements
- Information Gathering

Identify and communicate clear deliverables before the meeting starts

Use meeting invitations

36

Decision Making Criteria

- Company strategy
    - Aligned – how
    - Not – why not
- Long and short term goals
- Initiatives and projects
- Profitability
- Utilization/optimization of resources
- Efficiency, Evolution, Expertise
- Values
- Safety
- Compliance
- Other

Key Criteria

1.
2.
3.
& Gut check

A

B

Outline - Key Messages

1. What is important to my audience?
2. What are their drivers?
3. What are their concerns?
4. What are the tough questions they might ask?
5. What does success look like for them?

What are my Outcome(s)?

1. How do my 3 key messages address what is important to them?
2. Their drivers?
3. How will I address their needs and concerns?
4. What are my choices for responses?
5. What is the journey I want to take them on?

Put yourself in your audience's shoes and ask:
"What's really important to them?", "If they had that, what would having that do for them?"

38

Decisions in Computational Engineering Analysis

Three key points of the message:

1. Engineers face tough decisions in computational analysis.
2. Your decisions are crucial & you must be able to justify them. What if you are wrong?
3. You will be accountable! Act responsibly guided by good ethics.

My audience is a bunch of engineers who need to be put into a professional mindset.

Opening:
- Project Phoenix, P S did not document my work

Closing: - ESA broken structure.

Presentation Structure

Step 1:
High Impact Opening

- Get their attention
- Do something different, **"My name is and I am going to talk about...."** is not an option
- Establish credibility, confidence & approachability

High Impact Techniques

- Stories
- Metaphors and Similes
- Audience Participation
- Quotes
- Startling Statistics
- Facts

- One-liners
- Turn-a-phrase
- Music & Film Clips
- Props
- Charts

42

What is the story?

- Anecdotes and 'Signature' Stories
- Personal/self-disclosure
- Second hand
- 3rd person
- Famous people
- Humorous
- Dramatic
- Stories with a moral

Metaphors and Similes

Metaphors "is, was & are"

- Metaphor is defined as the substitution of one idea or object with another, used to assist expression or understanding.

Simile "as a & like a"

- Simile is an analogy that compares two things that are alike in one way.

44

Metaphors

- Humor is the shock absorber of life.
- This project is a slam dunk, a piece of cake.
- The problem is grist for the mill.
- He's a diamond in the rough.
- They are airheads.
- The clock is eating away our profits.
- Steve is a couch potato.
- That team is green … with envy.
- He is a steamroller
- She is a powerhouse.
- That estimate was the death of the idea
- Those words are bullets.
- Language is a road map of a culture.
- The needle that burst my balloon.
- He is a loose cannon.
- That project is dead weight.

Similes

- Busy as a bee
- Happy as a clam
- Blind as a bat
- They fought like cats and dogs
- Brave as a lion.
- Fought like cats and dogs.
- Funny as a barrel of monkeys.
- Clean as a whistle.
- Strong as an ox.
- Clear as mud.
- Was like watching grass grow.
- Solid as the ground we stand on.
- Nutty as a fruitcake.
- Don't just sit there like a bump on a log.
- That went over like a lead balloon.
- They are as different as night and day.
- She is as thin as a toothpick.
- Last night, I slept like a log.
- It fits like a glove.

Audience Participation

- Audience Response (vocal & non-verbal)
- Provocative Questions
- Dialogue & Interaction
- Demonstration
- Role-play
- Exercises

High Impact Techniques

Summary

- Stories
- Metaphors and Similes
- Audience Participation
- Quotes
- Startling Statistics
- Facts
- One-liners
- Turn-a-phrase
- Music & Film Clips
- Props
- Charts

Step 2:
Frame & WIIFM

- **Frame is the preview**
- **Keep it simple!**
- **WIIFM?**

- Why should they listen to you?
- What difference will it make to them?
- What impact will you have on the listeners?

Will it:

- Give them information,
- Add to their understanding,
- Help them make better decisions,
- Give them something they consider to be important?

49

Step 3:
The Key Points

- These are the 3 key elements of your presentation

- Think of a 3 legged stool

- Each of these points is like one of the legs – they are all needed to support the topic

Step 4:

Summary & Call to Action

- Optional for summarizing the main points

- The 'wrap up' of your talk

- This is where you 'ask for the order'

- If you are asking for a decision, urging action, or leaving them with a key thought in mind, this is the time to do it

Step 5:
High Impact Close

- "Bookend" your presentation by using the same metaphor to open and close.

- Use your same High Impact skills as your opener.

Presentation Structure

Design Your Presentation

1. High Impact Opening
2. Frame & WIIFM
3. 3 Key Points
4. Summary & Call to Action
5. High Impact Close

1. What high impact techniques
   - Stories
   - Metaphors and Similes
   - Audience Participation
   - Quotes
   - Startling Statistics
   - Facts
   - One-liners
   - Turn-a-phrase
   - Music & Film Clips
   - Props
   - Charts
2. Words
3. Vocalics
4. Gestures
5. Position

....
....
....
....
....
....
....
....
....
....
....
....
....
....
....
....
....
....
....
....
....
....
....
....

Notes

Cycle of Rapport

Calibration
(Read the other person)

Pacing
(Create the connection)

Leading
(Move toward your goal)

58

Calibration & Pacing

Visual Analog

- **Posture**
- **Gestures**
- **Facial Expressions**
- **'Energy'**
- **Breathing**
- **Attention**
- **Eye movements**

Auditory Digital

- **Key words and phrases**
- **Sensory words**

Auditory Analog

- **Volume**
- **Speed**
- **Pauses**
- **Pitch & Inflection**
- **Emotion**

59

Key Calibrations:

Yes/No

Agree/Disagree

Understanding/Confusion

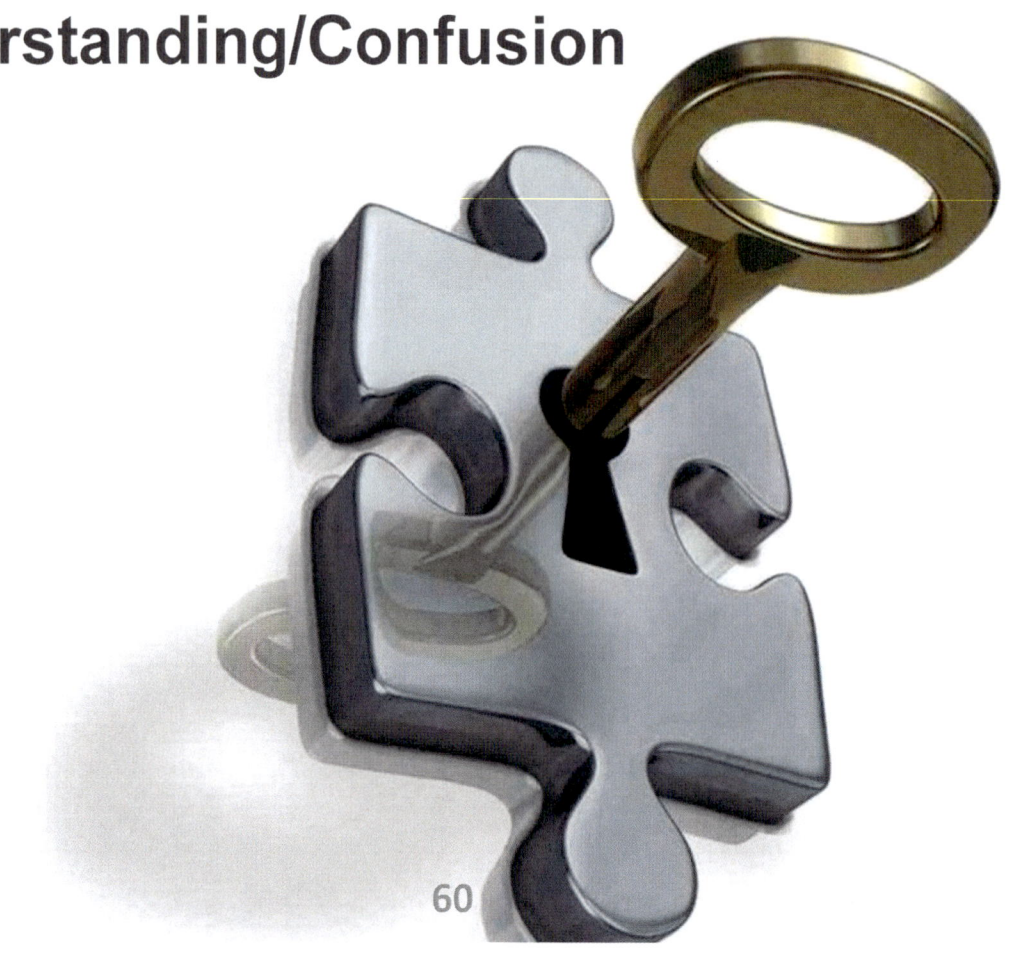

Rapport

- Utilize your own body and neurology
- Match and mirror elegantly
- Create an experience of comfort
- Understand from their perspective
- Gather information

Pacing

- Adjust when it is your turn to talk
- Make it natural, not "trying" to do something
- Start with obvious then to subtle
  - Posture & Gestures
  - Facial expressions
  - Key words & phrases

Map of Reality

Each person creates a map of reality that governs how they perceive the world, how they think & feel, how they make decisions, and they act

Study someone's map and you will know how to influence them

Eye Accessing Cues

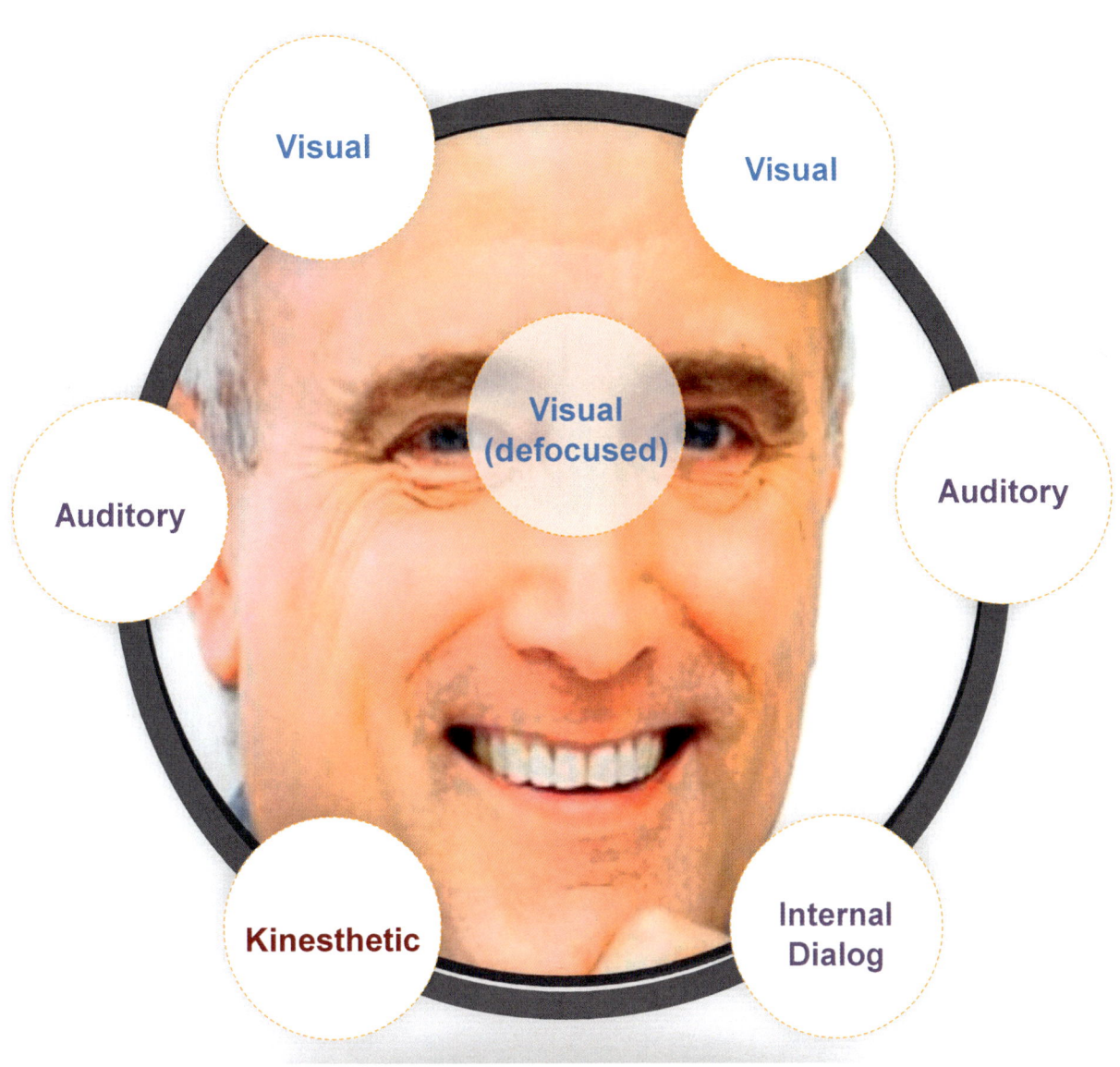

Visual Map

Processes in pictures & visuals

- Fast pace, high energy, talks fast in busts
- Gestures – Higher, points up
- Decisions – big picture, fast
- Vocals - high & rapid
- Breathing – high and rapid,
- Posture - upright
- Words – see, picture, bright, view, perspective, clear

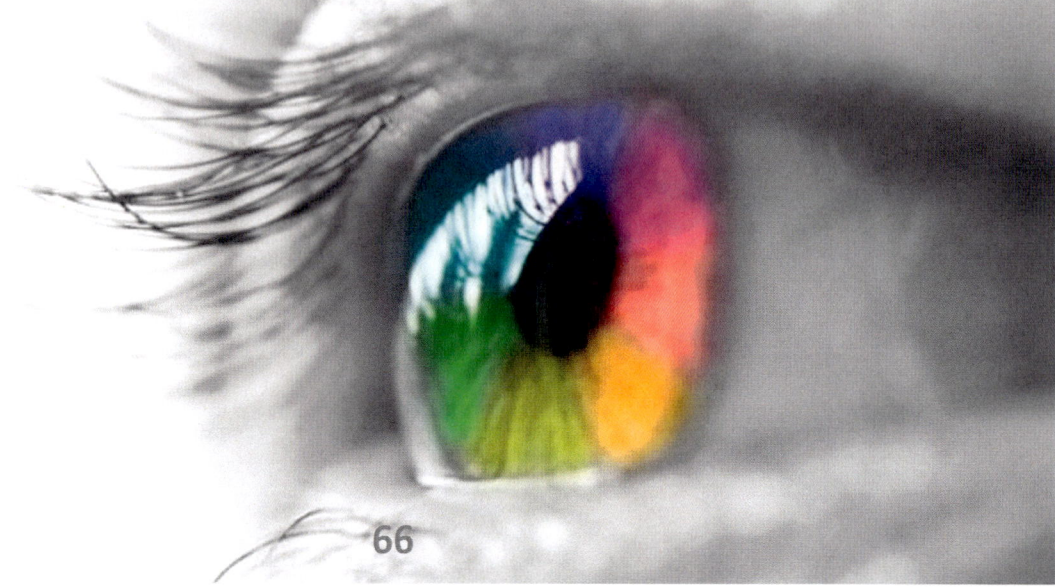

66

Kinesthetic Map

- Processes with sensations & movement
- Pauses, deliberate, finds words
- Gestures – lower, slower, touching
- Decisions – gut level, hunches, vibes
- Vocals – lower, slower, resonate, soft
- Breathing – abdominal
- Posture - leans
- Words – feel, handle, grasp, pick up, comfortable.

Auditory Map

Processes in dialog, sounds & stories

- Hears subtle meanings in language
- Gestures – mid-range, telephone gesture
- Decisions – detail analysis, wording
- Vocals – FM voice, or narrower monotone.
- Breathing – mid chest
- Words – listen, tell, speak, ring, harmony

Sensory Words

Visual	Kinesthetic	Auditory
See, pattern, focus neat, dim, portray, view light, look, dark appear, brilliant, scan observe, bright, reflect picture, spotless, sketch show, oversight, vision ugly, foggy, survey reveal, pretty, vie cloudy, strain, hazy visible, sight, glare shine, draw, glow watch, diagram, dull hide, clear, image blind, see, appear focus, perspective, picture clear, line of sight, bright	Unbalanced, feel, sting point, fumble, cool, hot soft, shocking, merge tender, bend, throw link, cram, tackle, fall, push, pack, shuffle, connect unite, catch, balance resist, sharp, twinge tough, cut, lift, touch, hurt, smooth, sturdy mold, support, stable attack, hard, cold, electric,, ragged, grasp, backing shape, grab, jarred rough, reach, attach firm, stiff , fasten, stick handle, twist, probe	Hear, talk, yell rasp, say, utter argue, sputter, whine shriek, compute, debate utter, lie, sing, complain babble, whine, growl tones, shriek, hiss, resounding, tell, discuss squeal, boom, chime snore, quiet, music praise, call, chant noise, purr, describe clatter, aloud, shrill ring, listen, voice scream, sound, loud mouth off, growl harmony, tell, silent mute, sing-song

69

LEADERSHIP

MINDSETS

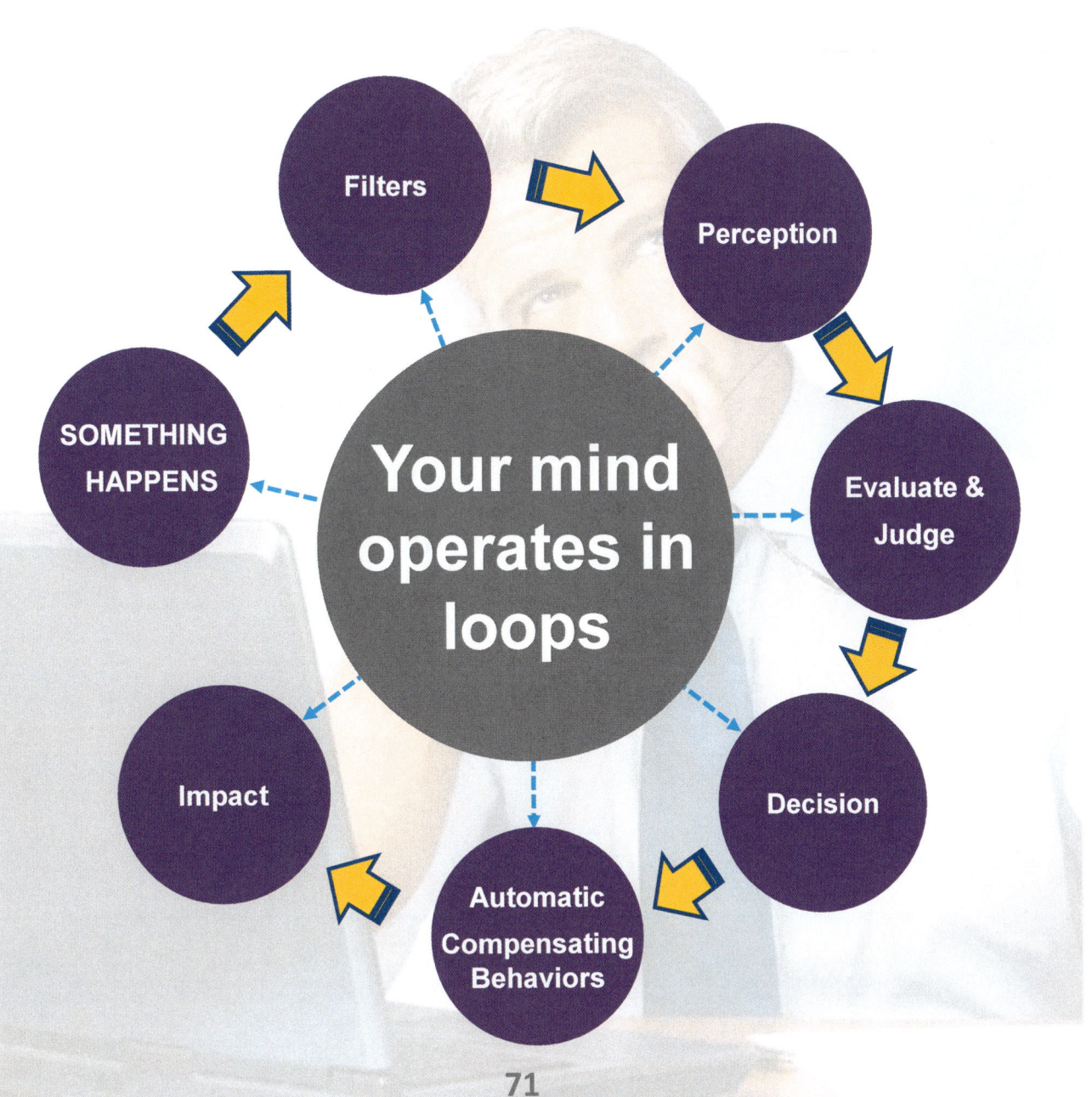

71

LEADERSHIP

What mindset are YOU OPERATING FROM?

DRAMA

MINDSET

EVENTS / ISSUES / CHALLENGES

What Triangle are You in?

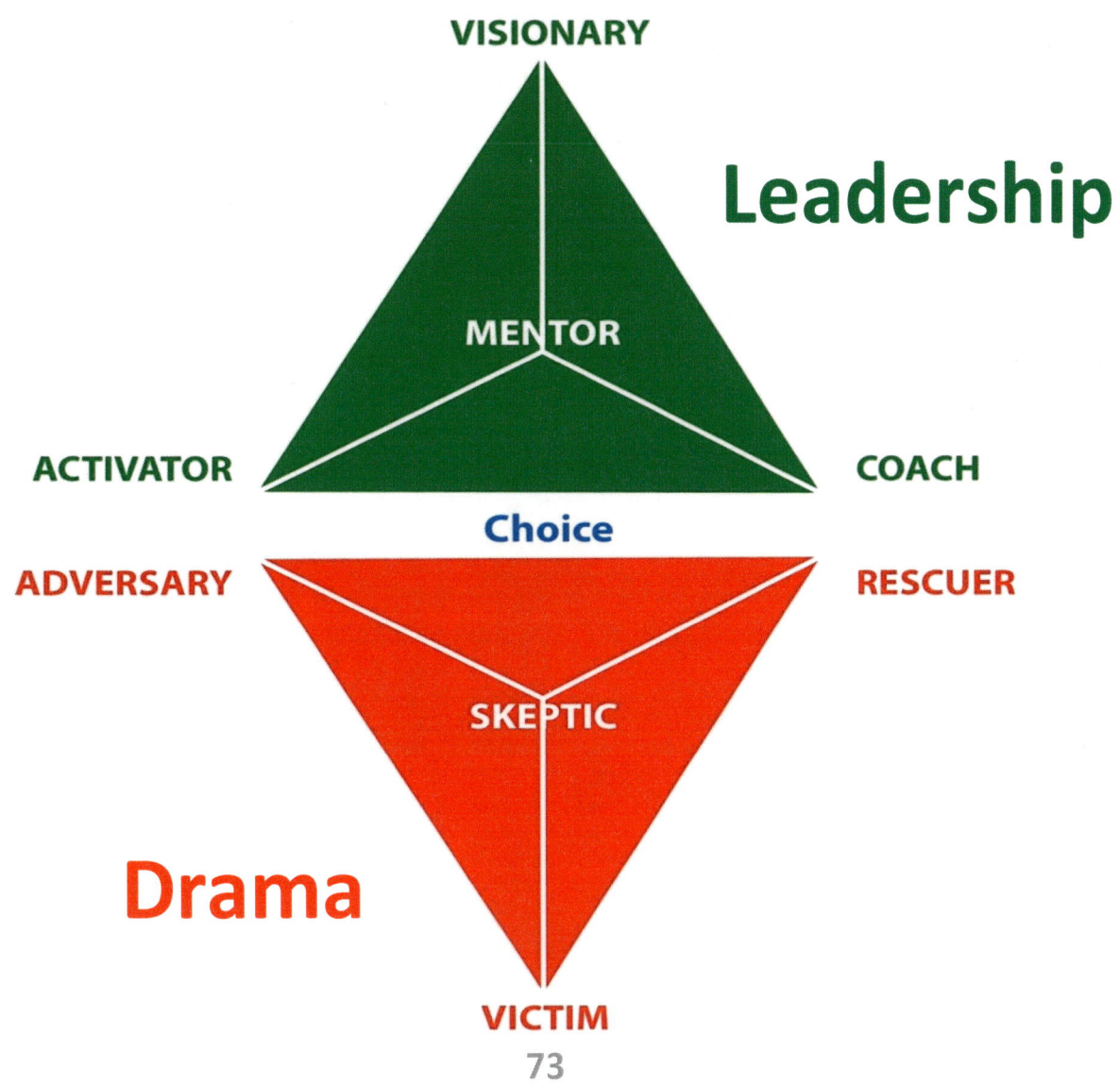

73

Check Your Attitude

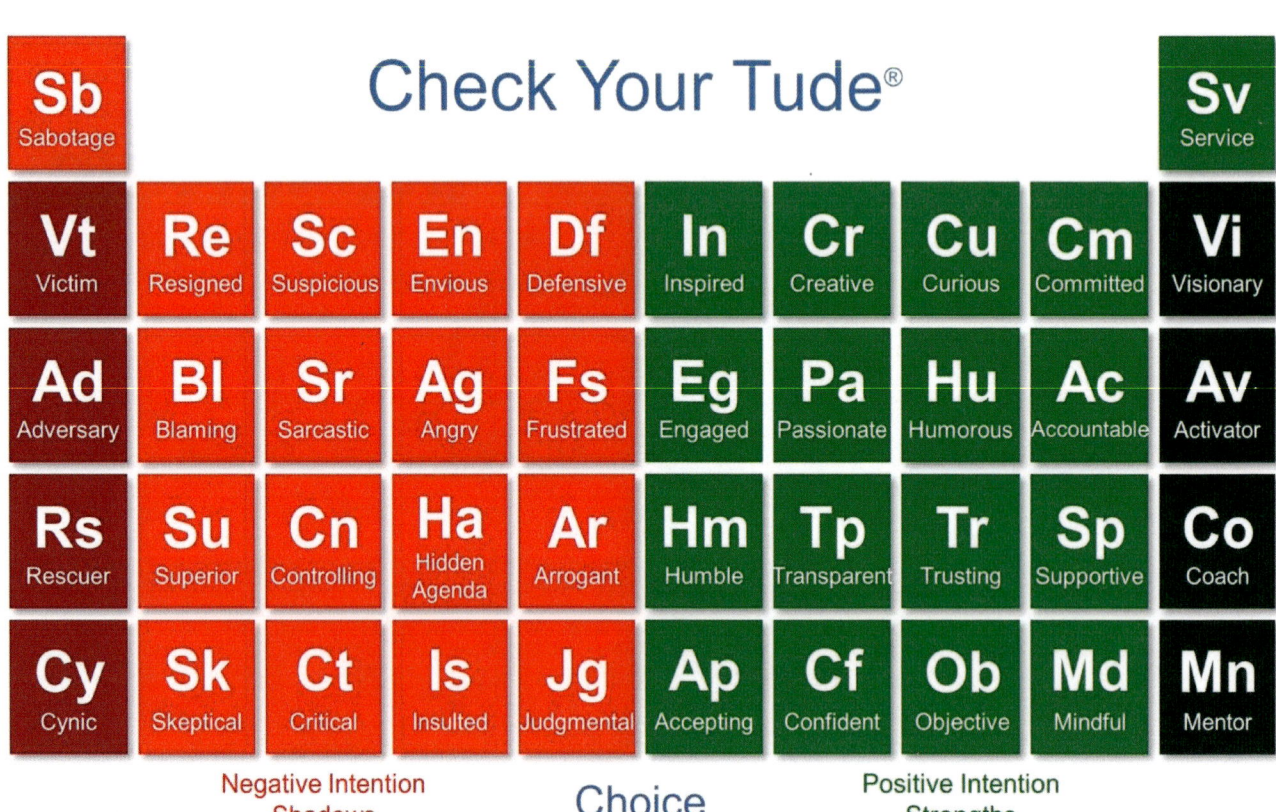

Check Your Tude®

Sb Sabotage									Sv Service
Vt Victim	Re Resigned	Sc Suspicious	En Envious	Df Defensive	In Inspired	Cr Creative	Cu Curious	Cm Committed	Vi Visionary
Ad Adversary	Bl Blaming	Sr Sarcastic	Ag Angry	Fs Frustrated	Eg Engaged	Pa Passionate	Hu Humorous	Ac Accountable	Av Activator
Rs Rescuer	Su Superior	Cn Controlling	Ha Hidden Agenda	Ar Arrogant	Hm Humble	Tp Transparent	Tr Trusting	Sp Supportive	Co Coach
Cy Cynic	Sk Skeptical	Ct Critical	Is Insulted	Jg Judgmental	Ap Accepting	Cf Confident	Ob Objective	Md Mindful	Mn Mentor

Negative Intention Shadows   Choice   Positive Intention Strengths

5 Steps to Check Your Attitude

1. Identify your **Positive Spin** strengths.

2. What situation/person triggers you to go into a **Negative Spin**?

• Where do you go?

• What is the thought or conclusion that starts you spinning in a negative way?

1. Step into **Choice**. Pause for a moment.

2. Take a few deep breaths to clear your upset and calm your thoughts.

3. Identify the **Positive** spin strengths that would be useful in that situation.

4. What would be different if you operated from that strength?

5. What reminder/anchor can you use to shift to the Positive strength in the future?

75

Circle of
Excellence

1. **Identify 2 – 3 strengths that you have.**
   - Color, texture, sound for each
2. **Put each into your circle on floor.**
3. **Enhance them.**
4. **Step into your circle & feel and absorb your strengths.**
5. **Create anchor/reminder for your strengths.**
6. **Identify situation in which you want to be more resourceful.**
7. **Take your strengths and step into that situation. Notice how it is.**

76

....
....
....
....
....
....
....
....
....
....
....
....
....
....
....
....
....
....
....
....
....
....
....
....

Notes

....
....
....
....
....
....
....
....
....
....
....
....
....
....
....
....
....
....
....
....
....
....
....
....
....

What makes us tick

Focus Areas– Inspiring Leaders, Exceptional Teams, Engaging Cultures, Alignment
Values – Positive Intention, Trust, Real Conversations, Growth

Inspiring Leaders –Inspiring leaders create an environment where people can be their best and exceed expectations. Inspiring leaders create **Trust** by being congruent role models who walk the talk. We work with leaders to evolve their ability to bring their intention, words, and actions into **Alignment**. Inspiring leaders choose **Positive Intention** as the foundation for how they approach others and their work. High performing leaders consistently work to balance their personal compliment of strengths and the strengths of those in their organization to bring out their best and support creativity, innovation and **Growth**.

Alignment - There is a 64 fold increase in the combined energy output of a team when you align the energies and people in your organization. We work with you to create the environment for people to voice their opinions, have robust debates/**Real Conversations,** and collaborate to create a way forward that is not dependent on everyone's agreement but is dependent on their buy-in.

Exceptional Teams – We are catalysts for leaders and their teams in establishing and sustaining a foundation of **Trust** and partnership. Members of **Exceptional Teams** engage in **Real Conversations**, the two-way exchanges based in **Positive Intention** where you are fully present and telling the truth in an engaging way that moves the action forward.

Engaging Cultures – Competitive business not only need to compete with each other they need to compete to engage and retain talent. An engaging culture supports **Growth** and development of the individual and to serve as a coach and mentor for others. Our purpose is to work with you to create an engaging culture though **Inspiring Leaders** and **Exceptional Teams** that will galvanize your workforce and truly be one of your *competitive advantages*.

LEADERSHIP
DEVELOPMENT GROUP

Jim Peal, PhD, CEO

Books on Amazon:

Check Your Attitude at the Door

Crocodiles at the Water Cooler

Daring to Have Real Conversations in Business

Leading Change

See Jim on TEDx Talks – "Decisions That Define Us"

Google Jim Peal TEDx talk

Oakland CA

Tel. (01) 805-966-3323

www.peal.com

www.leadershipDG.com

www.checkyourtude.com

Made in the USA
Columbia, SC
25 August 2019